~ A Lit

I R
FAMILY
NAMES

IDA GREHAN

Illustrated by Clare Williams

CHRONICLE BOOKS

SAN FRANCISCO

First published in 1997 by
The Appletree Press Ltd
19-21 Alfred Street
Belfast BT2 8DL
Tel. +44 (0)1232 243074
Fax +44 (0)1232 246756

A Little Book of Irish Family Names

First published in the United States in 1997
by Chronicle Books, 85 Second Street,
San Francisco, CA 94105

Web Site: www.chronbooks.com

ISBN 0-8118-1286-3

9 8 7 6 5 4 3 2 1

19391

Introduction

Tracing the family tree has a long history in Ireland where, in Celtic times, each family employed its own *seannachie*, or genealogist, to record the lines of descent. This little book focuses on the meaning, origin, locations and major personalities of fifty-six names, selected because they are among the most ancient, most influential, and most enduring of Irish families.

For convenience, the words sept and clan have been used interchangeably in this book, although strictly speaking it was the sept, rather than the clan, that was the dynastic system in Ireland. The sept comprised a group whose immediate ancestors had a common name, lived in the same locality, and who shared a common chieftain.

Hereditary surnames came spontaneously and comparatively early to Ireland in the 10th century. The prefix *Mac* meant son of, *O* could mean grandson or earlier ancestor, *Fitz* was from the French *fils*, meaning son. A girl added *Ni* before her father's name, while her mother prefixed *Ban*. Although these prefixes were sometimes dropped, they are still widely in use today.

With over forty million people in the United States claiming an Irish background, let alone those in Canada, Australia, New Zealand, Argentina, and elsewhere, it is little wonder that ancestor tracing has become such a large industry. Fortunately the Genealogical Office, founded in 1552 in Dublin Castle, is still in existence, located now in Kildare Street, Dublin. New American presidents still apply to it in search of their Irish ancestry!

Ahearne

Originally, this name was *Ó hEachighearna*, meaning lord of the house. It became O Hagerin in English, which in time changed to Ahern or Hearne. The name is originally Dalcassian, from a sept that migrated from east Clare to Co. Cork. In the 10th century this was an important sept, whose chieftain was Mathghamhain, King of Thomond, an elder brother of the Irish High King, Brian Boru. The territory of the King of Thomond at that time covered Co. Clare and parts of Co. Limerick. Today, there is no clan chief and no family seat. However, one place that has the name and many historical resonances is Hearn's Hotel in Clonmel, Co. Tipperary. Ireland's first ever public transport system started here in 1815, the Bianconi mail coach service.

Among well-known holders of the name was Patricio Lafacadio Hearn (1850–1904), a journalist who emigrated to Japan in 1890 and spent the rest of his life there. He explained Japan to the Western world, the first person to do so and, accordingly, is greatly honoured in Japan today.

Barry

This name is of Welsh-Norman origin and came from the name of the estate in Glamorgan in South Wales that belonged to Nesta (known as the Helen of Wales because of her many extramarital liaisons) and her husband, Gerald de Barri. Their son, Philip de Barri, came to Ireland with the Anglo-Norman invasion in 1170, and in 1179 he was granted extensive tracts of land in Munster. From that day to this, the name Barry has been principally associated with Co. Cork. The Barrys originally settled in north Co. Cork near Buttevant, named after the family motto *boutez en avant*, meaning "strike forward."

A Barry connection can also be seen in the delightful town of Bunclody in Co. Wexford. The town was bought by the Barry-Maxwell family in 1719 and, until 1950, was called Newtownbarry; then the name was changed to Bunclody, which in Irish means the mouth of the River Clody.

Blake

B lake is another Norman name of Welsh origin. Richard Caddell came to Ireland from Wales with the Normans in the 12th century. He was known as Niger or Le Blaca (the black one), which in time was transformed into Blake. The Blakes were one of the original Tribes of Galway, groupings of wealthy merchant families in Co. Galway. By the end of the 18th century, the Blakes had squandered their money and lost most of their estates.

William Blake (1757–1827), the English poet and mystic, was the son of an Irish hosier. Blake's life and work were unconventional, and his poetry was not appreciated until long after his death. In 1752 an amateur horse rider called Edward Blake challenged a neighbour to race him from Buttevant in north Co. Cork to Doneraile, four miles away, all the time keeping Doneraile steeple in sight. Thus was born the word *steeplechase*.

Browne

I n Connacht, Munster and Leinster, this name is usu-
ally spelled with an "e" on the end. It is Norman in
origin. A *Le Brun* came from Normandy and settled in
Co. Galway in the 12th century. An even earlier
Browne, Sir Philip Browne, had arrived with the Anglo-
Norman invasion in 1170 and become Governor of
Wexford. The name can also be traced back to the Old
English "Brun," which referred to hair, clothes, or com-
plexion. In Ulster, Brown is usually spelled without the
"e" and its origins there are quite different. This name
is an anglicisation of the Scots Gaelic, *Mac a' Bhruithin*
(son of the judge) or *Mac Gille Dhuinn* (son of the brown
boy).

Among the well-known Browns was William Brown,
born in Foxford, Co. Mayo, in 1777. In 1813, he became
closely involved with the struggle for Argentinian inde-
pendence and is regarded as the father of the
Argentinian Navy. He is duly commemorated in his
native Foxford, and in central Buenos Aires the main
square is called Plaza del Mayo, after his native county.

Burke

The name Burke, or *de Burgo*, is one of the most important and numerous of the Hiberno-Norman names. The first to arrive in Ireland was William FitzAlan de Burgo, who took his name from the town of Burgh in Suffolk. He arrived with the Anglo-Norman invasion.

In the early 17th century, Richard Burke built Portumna Castle in Co. Galway. It was the most magnificent house of its time in Ireland until gutted by fire in 1826, but its still impressive ruins can be freely seen today. Edmund Burke (1729–1797), whose statue is outside Trinity College, Dublin, was one of the most renowned philosophers of the 18th century, the father of the modern Conservative Party in Britain.

Places connected with the name include Burke's 17th-century pub in Clarinbridge, Co. Galway. Paddy Burke founded the famous oyster festival there in 1954. At Greencastle in Co. Donegal can be seen the ruins of the castle built by Richard de Burgo, the Red Earl of Ulster, in 1305 and destroyed in 1555.

Butler

The Butler name is of Norman origin; it originally meant wine steward and comes from the same root as the modern French word for bottle, *bouteille*. The Butlers arrived with the Anglo-Norman invasion in the 12th century, and in 1177 Theobald FitzWalter was made the Chief Butler of Ireland by King Henry II. Unlike many of the other Anglo-Norman names, it did not become gaelicised.

The most prominent Butler family in Ireland is descended from Theobald FitzWalter, and Kilkenny Castle is the most magnificent example still extant of a Butler residence. From the 14th to the 20th centuries, the castle was the main seat of the Earls and Dukes of Ormonde, who played a prominent part in Irish history. Other castles with strong Butler links include Cahir Castle; the Butlers came into possession of this castle in 1375 and it was taken from them in 1599.

Charles Butler, the 31st Chief Butler and 7th Marquess and Earl of Ossory, lives in Illinois.

Carroll

This name, which is particularly prevalent in the Co. Louth area of eastern Ireland, derives from the Irish word *cearbhaill*, which in its literal translation means slaughter but in a more acceptable translation means war-like champion. There were several different septs of the Carroll clan; the most important ones were those of Ely O'Carroll and Oriel, with minor septs in Co. Leitrim and Co. Kerry. A much older connection with the name can be seen in the village of Louth, eight miles southwest of Dundalk. Here can be seen the ruins of St. Mary's Abbey, built long before Anglo-Norman times and refurbished in 1148 by Donough O'Carroll, the Prince of Oriel, who also endowed Mellifont Abbey, just west of Drogheda.

One of the main fortresses of the O'Carrolls is Leap Castle, near Coolderry in Co. Offaly. The castle was burned during the Civil War in 1922 but the ruins are extensive. It is said to be the most haunted house in Ireland.

Clarke

This name has the same remote origins in Ireland, England, and Scotland. The Latin word *clericus* originally meant clergyman and then came to mean clerk or scholar. In Irish, the word *cléireach* was anglicised in translation to Clarke. Until the end of the 19th century, the names Cleary and Clarke were interchangeable in some parts of the country. The O'Clery name was originally found in Co. Galway and later became widespread in counties Donegal and Derry.

The Clarkes were noted as poets and antiquarians. The most famous person to hold the name was Austin Clarke (1896–1974), one of Ireland's most outstanding poets. In Bordeaux, Château Clarke, a leading vineyard in the region, was developed by Luc Tobie Clarke, a great-grandson of James Clarke, who was an alderman of Dublin City in 1688. Harry Clarke was one of the most renowned Irish artists in stained glass in the 20th century. His work can be seen in innumerable churches and convents around Ireland and in Bewley's cafe in Grafton Street, Dublin.

Collins

This name is derived from a diminutive of Nicholas. The Gaelic version of the name is *Ó Coileáin*, which means a young dog. Until the 13th century, the clan were lords of the barony of Connello in Co. Limerick and today the name remains common in both Co. Limerick and Co. Cork.

Two place-names in Ireland derive their name from Collins: Collinstown is the site of Dublin airport and for many years the airport was referred to simply as Collinstown; in Co. Westmeath, Collinstown is a small crossroads village not far from Lough Lene.

The most famous holder of the name was Michael Collins (1890–1922), born at Woodfield, near Clonakilty, Co. Cork. He was closely involved in the War of Independence, where many of his exploits were legendary, and then in the Anglo-Irish negotiations that resulted in the 1921 treaty. He was killed at Béal na mBláth in west Cork in 1922. This site, and also his birthplace, are preserved.

Connolly

T his name is common in all four provinces of Ireland. In Irish, it is *Ó Conghaile*, which means valorous. Although so widely distributed, the origins of this name are in Co. Monaghan and in Connacht.

Among well-known Connollys were William Connolly, the richest man in Ireland in the 18th century. A lawyer and financier, he made his fortune buying and selling land lost by the old Gaelic families exiled after the Battle of the Boyne. He was also Speaker in the Irish Parliament. In 1722, he built Castletown House at Celbridge, Co. Kildare, one of Ireland's finest mansions. Restoration is nearly complete and it can be visited.

James Connolly (1870–1916) was one of the leaders of the 1916 Easter Rising and the pioneer of socialism in Ireland. Sybil Connolly, born in 1921, has achieved international fame with her fashion designs; her work-rooms are in Merrion Square, Dublin.

Daly

Daly is one of the oldest and most heroic of all Irish family names. The Dalys claim descent from one of Ireland's epic heroes from Celtic mythology, Niall of the Nine Hostages. He was the High King of Tara from A.D. 380 to 405. The Hill of Tara can still be seen today, an impressive sight, even though the remains of the royal palaces there are long gone.

The name Daly comes from the Irish word *dáil*, which means a place where councils or assemblies are held. The present day Dáil (lower house of parliment in Dublin) has this same meaning.

Originally, the Dalys were to be found in Co. Westmeath, but there were sub-septs in many different localities in counties Clare, Cork, and Galway. There are now more than 30,000 Dalys in Ireland. The name is also known as Dawley.

In the 19th century, Marcus Daly, from Ballyjamesduff in Co. Cavan, who emigrated to California, became enormously wealthy from his mining activities and was nicknamed the "Copper King."

Dillon

D illons have always played a prominent part in Irish history. The name is of Hiberno-Norman origins and is particularly widespread in counties Meath, Roscommon, and Westmeath. In Co. Westmeath, the Dillons once owned so much land that it was referred to as Dillon's County.

The first person to come to Ireland with the name was Sir Henry de Leon, from a small town of the same name in Britanny, France. He arrived in 1185, immediately after the Anglo-Norman invasion, to act as secretary to Prince, later King, John of England and France. Over the years, the name has become accepted as an Irish rather than a Norman name: in Irish, Dillon is *Ó Duilleáin*.

The present representative of the Viscomtes Dillon, a title created in 1622, is Henry, 22nd Viscount of Costello-Galen and Count of France. He was born in 1973 and lives in London.

Doherty

This name is still very much connected with Co. Donegal in north-west Ireland and is one of the oldest hereditary surnames in the country. In Irish, the name means obstructive. The Dohertys are descended from one of the eight sons of Niall of the Nine Hostages, who ruled at Tara at the beginning of the 5th century. The present head of the clan and the 37th Doherty chieftain is Dr. Ramón Salvador O'Doherty, who lives in Cadiz in southern Spain.

Despite the name being so common in Donegal, ruins associated with the clan are somewhat sparse. However, in Buncrana, the keep still remains of the castle built c. 1430 by the O'Doherty clan. The castle was burnt by the English in 1602 when the Irish chieftain Hugh Boy O'Doherty was preparing to welcome an armada from Spain.

Among the famous Dohertys was John Doherty, from Buncrana, the most renowned trade union leader in early-19th-century Britain. He founded the National Association of United Trades for the Protection of Labour, a forerunner of the Trades Union Congress.

Doyle

D oyle is one of the most numerous family names in Leinster, especially around Wexford. The origins of the name are unclear but are believed to come from the nickname given to the Viking invaders of Ireland in about the 9th century. They were called *dubh-ghall*, which means dark foreigner. This name was changed over the years to become Doyle.

Some of this name have made distinctive contributions to the arts. Sir Arthur Conan Doyle (1859–1930), famous for writing about that great character of detective fiction, Sherlock Holmes, was born in Edinburgh of an Irish Catholic family. His uncle, Richard Doyle, was a well-known contributor to *Punch* magazine in the mid-19th century. In modern times, Roddy Doyle, born in Dublin in 1958, has achieved worldwide fame and wealth from such novels as *The Commitments* and *Paddy Clarke, Ha, Ha, Ha*. Jack Doyle (1913–1978) was known as the Gorgeous Gael; a boxer and playboy who achieved fame, not to say notoriety, during and after World War II.

Duffy

T his name is now the single most common name in Co. Monaghan, where it originated. Its Irish version is *Ó Dubthaigh*, which means black, probably referring to hair. In Ulster, Dowey is a common variant.

One of the most notorious holders of this name from Co. Monaghan was General Eoin O'Duffy, Chief Commissioner of the Garda Siochana (the Irish police force) after independence. He was sacked from his position by the incoming de Valera government in the early 1930s and went on to found the extreme right-wing, fascist-style organisation popularly known as the Blueshirts.

An earlier Duffy with an altogether more heroic career was Sir Charles Gavan Duffy (1816–1903), Premier of the colony of Victoria, Australia. He, too, was born in Monaghan town. The American actor Patrick Duffy achieved worldwide fame in the 1980s as the character Bobby Ewing in the TV series *Dallas*.

Egan

This name originated in Co. Galway and in south Co. Roscommon. It is a pared-down anglicisation of the ancient Gaelic surname *Mac Aodhagáin*, which means son of Hugh, and was also used to denote a pagan fire deity. Over the years, the name changed to Egan, which in some parts of the country, particularly in Dublin and Wicklow, has been changed further to Keegan.

An early clan member was Owen MacEgan (1570–1603), a militant bishop who encouraged a Spanish invasion of Ireland in 1602. The Spanish landed in Kenmare, Co. Kerry. He was killed six months later and is buried in the convent grounds at Timoleague, Co. Cork.

The clan seat is Redwood Castle at Lorrha in Co. Tipperary, near the north-east corner of Lough Derg and the town of Portumna. The fine castle here was originally built about 1210 and in recent times has been carefully restored by Michael J. Egan from Castlebar, Co. Mayo. The Egan clan rally is now held here every year; the first such rally was in 1982.

FitzGerald

The FitzGeralds are one of the two greatest families that came to Ireland with the Anglo-Norman invasion in the 12th century. The name means simply son of Gerald and may have its origins in Italy, with the medieval Gherardini family of Florence. They crossed Europe to settle in Wales and then came to Ireland in the 12th century.

There are two main divisions of the FitzGeralds: the Desmond branch and the Kildare branch. The name can be found in many parts of Ireland but is most numerous in counties Cork, Kerry, Kildare, and Limerick. Among the places associated with the FitzGeralds is Kilkea Castle, near Athy in Co. Kildare. It was once the residence of a branch of the FitzGeralds, the Dukes of Leinster, but is now a luxury hotel.

Glin Castle, eight miles west of Foynes, on the southern shores of the Shannon estuary, is open to the public. This is the seat of Desmond FitzGerald, 29th Knight of Glin, whose family has been in continuous possession of the castle for 700 years.

Healy

There were two distinct septs, or clans, of the Healys. The first of these derived their name from the Irish *eilidhe*, meaning claimant, and were based around Lough Arrow in Co. Sligo. The other and very different sept, which was centred on the barony of Muskerry in Co. Cork, derived its name from *Ó hEalaighthe*, meaning ingenious. Their name was sometimes anglicised as Healihy.

One outstanding place associated with the name is Knocklofty House, just outside Clonmel in Co. Tipperary. This great mansion, built in the 18th century, was home of the Hely Hutchinsons, who had close links with both the Bank of Ireland and Guinness. They were also the Earls of Donoughmore.

Another spot connected with the Healy name is the Healy Pass on the Beara peninsula in west Cork. It is perhaps the most magnificent and desolate scenic drive in Ireland, built in the 1920s at the insistence of Tim Healy, who wanted to create employment in the district.

Hennessy

This family name, forever associated with brandy, comes from the Irish *Ó hAonghusa*, which is derived from the word *aonghus*, meaning choice. The leading sept, or clan, was based near Kilbegan in Co. Offaly. With the arrival of the Normans in 1170 they scattered to Limerick, Tipperary, and Cork, where many of the name are still to be found.

Hennessy brandy was first distilled by Richard Hennessy (1720–1800), who was born in Ballymacmoy House near Mallow in north Co. Cork. He went to France in 1740 and became an officer in Dillon's Irish Regiment in the French Army. In 1765, he went to the Charente département and set up the distillery that produces Hennessy brandy. The distillery continues to this day, as does the Hennessy line in the company. The Hennessy house at Killavullen near Mallow, overlooking the River Blackwater, can still be seen today.

Higgins

H iggins is another family name with ancient royal connections. This name is an anglicisation of *Ó hUigin*, from *uiginn*, meaning Viking. The word also means knowledge, skill or ingenuity. The original holder of the name was a grandson of Niall of the Nine Hostages, a High King of Tara. There is also a later English derivation too; Higgins as an English name comes from the medieval name Higgin, which was a diminutive of Hicke, a pet name given to anyone called Richard. In medieval Ireland, the Higgins were a sept, or clan, of the southern Uí Neills, who settled in Connacht, especially around Co. Sligo.

The most famous holder of the name was Bernardo O'Higgins (1778–1842), the first president of Chile and the founder of the Chilean Navy. The main street in Santiago is called Avenida O'Higgins in honour of the man who gave Chile its independence from Spain. O'Higgins was the son of Ambrosio O'Higgins, who came from a poor rural background near Summerhill in Co. Meath.

Joyce

The family name Joyce has both ancient Irish and Norman antecedents. It comes from a Brehon penal name (the Brehon laws were the ancient laws of Ireland, before Christian times). The Brehon name *Iodoc* is a diminutive of *iudh*, which means lord. It was adopted by the Normans in the form *Josse*. The first Norman bearer of the name in Ireland was Thomas de Joise, a Welsh Norman who settled in Connacht on the borders of counties Galway and Mayo toward the end of the 12th century. The name may also have been derived from the Norman personal name *Joie*, which means joy.

The continuation of the Joyce name in the west of Ireland can be seen to this day in the area of Connemara known as Joyce's Country. Many people with the name still live there, and Renvyle House, now a luxury hotel, was once a Joyce stronghold. The most famous Joyce is, of course, James Joyce, born in Dublin in 1882, who died in Zurich in 1941. He is widely acclaimed as the leading writer in the English language in the 20th century.

Kavanagh

The Kavanaghs have a royal lineage and some of them have had distinguished if rumbustious careers. Diarmiud MacMurrough was the 12th-century King of Leinster. He was notorious for inviting the Anglo-Norman invasion of Ireland. His son Donal, in order to distinguish him from other Donals when he was being educated in Wexford, was called *Caomhanach* (of St. Kevin's church), which was anglicised to Kavanagh.

Donal did not become a king but did acquire large tracts of land in Wexford and Carlow, which remain strongholds of the Kavanaghs to this day. Borris House in Co. Carlow was once a MacMurrough-Kavanagh house and is being restored. In Co. Wexford, the MacMurrough-Kavanagh connection is maintained in two castles: Ferns Castle was owned and occupied by the family from 1402 to 1550, and the castle in Enniscorthy, now the Wexford county museum, was once also a MacMurrough-Kavanagh stronghold. The Kavanaghs were Kings of Leinster until Henry VIII's reign in the 16th century.

Kennedy

In Irish, Kennedy is *Ó Cinnéide*, which means ugly-headed or rough-headed. The original holder of the Kennedy name was a nephew of the Irish king Brian Boru, who defeated the Norsemen at the Battle of Clontarf in 1014 and was then killed himself. The ancestral homeland of the Kennedys is in north Tipperary, east Clare and down into south Wexford.

Of all the Kennedys, John F. Kennedy (1917–1963), President of the United States, was the most famous. He was able to trace his direct ancestry back to Co. Wexford. The Kennedy homestead at Dunganstown, near New Ross, can still be visited, while the nearby Kennedy Memorial Park was created in his memory after he was assassinated in Dallas in 1963, just five months after his triumphant visit to Ireland.

Jimmy Kennedy (1902-1984) from Omagh, Co. Tyrone, was a world-famous songwriter. He composed such songs as "Red Sails in the Sunset," inspired by a sunset over Portstewart strand in Co. Antrim, and "Teddy Bear's Picnic."

Kirwin

This family name is of Gaelic origin, but they claim descent from Heremon, a son of the King of Spain, who conquered Ireland in the 6th century B.C. The name is frequently spelt Kirwan.

The Kirwan stronghold has always been in Co. Galway, and they were one of the Tribes of Galway, wealthy merchant families who ruled the city in medieval times. The family captured Castlebracket in Co. Galway, rebuilt it several times, but finally sold it in 1986. Otherwise, the Kirwans did not build any outstanding castles.

The Kirwans are also connected with the Bordeaux wine region in France. An English merchant, Sir John Collingwood, bought a château and vineyards here in 1751. His daughter married Mark Kirwan from Galway. He was beheaded in the French Revolution, but the family managed to hold onto the estates. Château Kirwan is still going strong today, but is owned largely by an insurance company.

Lynch

The name can be traced back to Labradh Longseach, who was ruler of Ireland for eighteen years from 541 B.C. *Longseach* means mariner. There are two quite separate Lynch septs, or clans. In addition to the ancient Irish sept, there's a Norman one, too. The de Lenchs came to Ireland with the Anglo-Norman invasion; it is thought that this branch of the family is descended from the great emperor Charlemagne, who conquered most of western Christendom in A.D. 800. The family had connections with Linz in Austria and migrated westwards.

While the Lynchs are common in counties Antrim, Down, Cavan, Clare, Cork, and Tipperary, they are particularly connected with Co. Galway, where they were one of the famous Tribes of Galway. In the centre of Galway city stands Lynch's Castle, a fine mansion dating back to 1320. Once the residence of the Lynch family, it is now a bank branch. The history of the family is well detailed inside the building.

MacCarthy

The name comes from the Irish MacCarthaigh, derived from *carthach*, which means loving. The original Carthach was King of Cashel in Co. Tipperary about 1040.

In Co. Cork, the famous Blarney Castle, where visitors can be blessed with the gift of the gab, was originally a MacCarthy stronghold. The castle was built in 1446 by Cormac MacCarthy and was owned by the family until the early 17th century.

In north Co. Cork, just outside the town of Kanturk, are the impressive ruins of Kanturk Castle, begun c. 1601 by a local chieftain, MacDonagh MacCarthy. It was to have been the biggest house ever built for an Irish chieftain, but the British government ordered a halt to the construction work. MacCarthy was so annoyed that he smashed all the blue glass tiles that had been made for the roof, and the castle was left unfinished, without roof or floors.

The present head of the family is Terence MacCarthy Mór, born in Belfast in 1957, a painter living mainly in Tangier in Morocco.

MacDermot

This name comes from Muiredach Mullethan, who was King of Connacht from 697 to 702. The name is spelled in different ways: McDermott-Roe, MacDermot, and Dermody, while in the United States it's Kermode. The area around Lough Key in Co. Roscommon used to be a MacDermot stronghold. The Cistercian abbey at nearby Boyle was also under the patronage of the MacDermots and no fewer than thirteen heads of this family are buried there.

A famous legend is connected with Lough Key. Una Bhan MacDermot and Thomas Láidir McCostello were ill-fated lovers from rival families. Una's family confined her to Castle Island, where she became ill and died. McCostello swam out to her grave every night until he, too, died. The two lovers were buried together, and two rose-trees over their graves became entwined. Those trees are still there today.

The MacDermots are the only family in Ireland to have added the courtesy title of Prince to their name. The current head of the principal branch of the family is Niall MacDermot, Prince of Coolavin.

MacGrath

Originally, this name was MacCraith, which means son of Raith (*raith* meaning prosperity). One McGrath sept, or clan, was based in counties Donegal and Fermanagh, the other in counties Clare and Limerick. In the 16th century a McGrath from the Donegal and Fermanagh sept built Castle Magrath at Pettigo near Lough Derg, and the McGraths were guardians of the monastery at Lough Derg.

There are various links with the MacGrath name around Dungarvan, Co. Waterford. In the town itself, what is known as Abbeyside, or McGrath's Castle, dates from the 12th or 13th century. Only the west wall remains. In the nearby ruins of the 13th-century Augustinian priory is a tomb with the inscription "Donald McGrath, 1490." He was one of the Co. Waterford sept, which had migrated there from Clare and Limerick.

In Co. Down, the name is usually spelled as "McGraw."

MacGuinness

Τhis family name originated in Iveagh, in what is now Co. Down. From the 12th to the 17th centuries, the seat of power was the town of Rathfriland in Co. Down. Here the Magennises (another spelling of MacGuinness) had their main castle, which was destroyed in 1641. The name comes from the Irish, meaning son of Aonghus (*aongus* means one choice), and can be traced back to the 5th century and the time of St. Patrick: the sept was descended from Saran, Chief of Dal Araidhe (Dalriada), an ancient territory of the North.

The name often has Northern connections. The Guinness family of brewing fame was originally from Co. Down. Richard Guinis was the agent to the Protestant Archbishop of Cashel in Co. Tipperary. Hop plants growing in the grounds of the Archbishop's Palace were used by Guinis to produce the dark-coloured beer that his son Arthur brewed when he started the world-famous St. James's Gate brewery in Dublin in 1759.

MacGuire

This family name comes from the Irish *Mag Uidhir*, which means pale. By the end of the 12th century, the MacGuires were the leading sept in Co. Fermanagh.

Two castles in the county were MacGuire strongholds. Enniskillen Castle, still in good repair, was at the heart of the 15th-century settlement established by Hugh the Hospitable and a stronghold of the ruling Maguire family. Information about the clan and its history can be found here. Tully Castle, overlooking Lower Lough Erne, was sacked by Rory Maguire and a band of his followers in 1641. They spared the Humes, who were inside, but murdered the other occupants. The ruins of this castle can still be explored.

The present head of the Maguires of Fermanagh is Terence Maguire, born in 1926, who lives in Dublin. His laudable aim is to bring together the Irish clans and, in so doing, help heal the wounds of Irish history. The names MacGuire and Maguire have the same origins.

MacKenna

This sept, or clan, is a branch of the southern Uí Neills. The name is found mainly in Co. Monaghan but is also numerous in Leinster. In Irish the name means son of Cionnaith. Despite being one of the most common surnames in Ireland, little is known about the origins of the family.

Among the famous bearers of the name is the actress Siobhan McKenna (1923–1986). She was born in Belfast and became one of the most outstanding Irish actresses of her generation. Another foremost contemporary actor is T. P. McKenna, who was born in Mullagh, near Virginia, Co. Cavan, in 1929.

A McKenna figure of note in history was General Juan MacKenna, who was born in Ireland in 1771. Where he was born remains something of a mystery; some sources claim he was born just outside Monaghan town, the true home of the McKennas, while others say that he was born in Clogher, Co. Tyrone. He was a famous soldier of fortune in Chile but died in 1814 in Buenos Aires, where he is buried.

MacMahon

This name comes from *Mac Mathuna*, which means son of a bear. It was first used by the son of Murtagh Mór, an O'Brien king of Ireland, who died in A.D. 119. Traditionally, this sept was associated with Co. Clare: there's a 15th-century tomb of the McMahon family in Ennis Friary at Ennis, and at Loop Head the ruins of Carrigaholt Castle, a McMahon stronghold, can still be seen. The other sept of the MacMahons is connected with Co. Monaghan.

One noted McMahon was Maura Rua MacMahon, whose husband, Conor O'Brien, was killed by Cromwellian forces in 1651. They lived in Leamaneh Castle, near Kilfenora in Co. Clare. When enemy soldiers brought back her husband's body from the battlefield, she is said to have shouted at them from a window of the castle: "Take him away. We want no dead men here!"

In the 19th century, Edmonde Patrice MacMahon (1808–1893) became a President of France. The Château de Sully, near Orléans, is the home of the present Philippe MacMahon, the fourth Duke of Magenta and a direct descendant of the former President.

MacNamara

This family name is closely connected with Co. Clare and is the most important sept of Dál gCais—ancient Irish chieftains dating back to prehistoric times—after the O'Briens of this county. The name comes from Mac Conmara, meaning son of the hound of the sea, Co. Clare being on the Atlantic coast. Several castles have connections with the MacNamaras, including Bunratty Castle, near Shannon airport. The MacNamaras owned Bunratty Castle before it passed to the O'Briens. Knappogue Castle, nearby, was built by a MacNamara in 1487. Also in this part of Co. Clare is Cratloe Castle, built by the MacNamaras in 1610.

The most important site in Co. Clare associated with the MacNamaras is Quin Abbey, six miles east of Ennis. The abbey was founded by Sioda MacNamara in 1402 and contains tombs of the MacNamara family.

Francis McNamara, who died in 1945, owned the Falls Hotel in Ennistymon, Co. Clare, a delightful village with some shop signs still in Irish and the ever-present falls. He was the father of Caitlín, who married the drunken but melodic Welsh poet Dylan Thomas.

MacSweeney

The Sweeneys trace their ancestry back to Niall of the Nine Hostages, a 5th-century High King of Ireland. The sept was very much of Donegal origin, but it wasn't until the 14th century that three great septs of the Tirconnell MacSweeneys were established. More than a century later, a branch of the clan went to Munster, and today the name is quite widespread in counties Cork and Kerry.

The principal seat of the MacSweeneys in Donegal is Doe Castle, near Creeslough in north Donegal, dating from the early 15th century. Rahan Castle, near Killybegs in Co. Donegal, was another MacSweeney clan stronghold.

The present head of the Fanad, Co. Donegal, Sweeneys is Chevalier Loughlin Sweeney, a Dublin bank manager. The head of the family in Spain is Doña Mary de Navascues, the Marquisa de Casacagal. Her Sweeney forebears were Spanish governors of Cuba. In Canada, the Sweeney clan is represented by Captain Richard Mingo Sweeney, whose family emigrated from Co. Tipperary in 1830.

Malone

The name originally came from the Irish name *Ó Maoil Eoin*. Maol is Irish for bald and refers to the tonsures sported by Irish monks. The name also means servant of St. John.

The Malones are an offshoot of the O'Connors of Connacht and their early history is centred around Offaly. In the early Middle Ages, Clonmacnoise, that splendid ecclesiastical site near the River Shannon, not far from Athlone, had a number of Malone abbots and bishops. The site is well preserved and has an informative visitors centre.

The best-known Malone had her origins in 18th-century Dublin street life. Molly Malone was a real fishwife, and the famous song, "Sweet Molly Malone", with its references to cockles and mussels, is a song about a real person. A statue of her can be seen at the foot of Grafton Street in Dublin. In popular Dublin parlance, she's referred to as "The Tart with the Cart."

Martin

Martin, or Martyn, is one of the most numerous names in Ireland, England, and Scotland. The name is also an abbreviation of Gilmartin. The Martins came to Ireland with the Anglo-Norman invasion and became prominent in the west where they were one of the Tribes of Galway. One of the Martin family in Co. Galway claims direct descent from Olyver Martin, who was a Crusader under King Richard II.

Martins have been prominent in the arts. Edward Martyn, who lived at Tulira Castle, Co. Galway, was a founder of the Abbey Theatre, Dublin, in 1896. Violet Martin was born at Ross in Co. Galway and teamed up with her cousin Edith Somerville to produce wonderfully amusing tales of Anglo-Irish life, including *Some Experiences of an Irish RM*.

Richard Martin (1754–1834) was known as Humanity Dick; he founded the Royal Society for the Prevention of Cruelty to Animals. His family owned Ballynahinch Castle in Connemara, where his estates stretched for thirty miles from his front door, giving him the longest avenue in Europe. The Martin castle is now a hotel.

Murphy

The most numerous name in Ireland, Murphy is derived from *Ó Murchada* or *Ó Murchu*, meaning sea warrior. There are several septs, or clans, of Murphys. The most famous Murphy was Dermot MacMurrough, who invited the Normans to Ireland in the 12th century. The present chief of the name is David O'Morchoe, a farmer in Co. Wexford. The Irish version of Murphy was first anglicised to O'Morchoe, in the 16th century, and David O'Morchoe's grandfather changed his name to this version by deed poll in 1895.

The achievements of the Murphy clan are numerous and wide ranging. Patrick Murphy, born in Co. Down in 1832, was the tallest man in Europe, standing at 8 ft. 1 in. Another Murphy of repute was William Martin Murphy. He founded the *Irish Independent* newspaper in 1905, and was also the head of the company that ran the Dublin tramway system. He became notorious as the employers' leader in the great Dublin lockout of 1913.

Nolan

Nolan comes from *Nuall*, which means nobleman, and is a name that goes back to the mists of early Irish history. It is numerous in all provinces but especially in Connacht and south-east Leinster. It is particularly connected with Co. Carlow. The head of the family was the Prince of Foharta (now known as Forth) in Co. Carlow.

Among the famous holders of the name was Brian O'Nolan (1911–1966), who was born in Strabane, Co. Tyrone, but was educated and lived for the rest of his life in Dublin. A senior civil servant by day, he wrote the satirical Cruiskeen Lawn column for *The Irish Times* and a number of books, including *The Third Policeman*, *The Dalkey Archive*, and *At Swim–Two Birds*. He wrote under the names of Flann O'Brien and Myles na gCopaleen. Another distinguished member of the clan was Sir Robert Sidney Nolan (1917–92), the Australian painter, born to Irish immigrant parents in Melbourne.

Nugent

The Nugent family name has Norman origins and is widespread in counties Cork and Westmeath. The man who brought the name to Ireland was Hugh de Nugent, who arrived with the Anglo-Norman invasion in the 12th century. His family name came from the town of Nugent-le-Rotrou, near Chartres in France.

Two castles in Co. Westmeath had connections with the Nugents. Ballinlough Castle, at Clonellan, was saved from destruction in the 1930s by Sir Hugh Nugent and is still in Nugent occupation, while Delvin Castle, in the same county, was a Nugent stronghold.

Christopher Nugent, Baron Delvin, wrote the *Irish Primer* for Queen Elizabeth I. Count Lavall Nugent (1777–1862) from Ballincor, Co. Wicklow, was a field marshal in the Austrian army. He was present at the Battle of Solferino in 1859 at the age of eighty-two years. Frank Nugent was the deputy leader of the Irish Everest expedition in 1993, and Barbara Nugent is chief executive of the *Sunday Business Post* newspaper in Dublin.

O'Brien

O'Brien, one of most renowned of all Irish names, comes from Brian Boru, High King of Ireland in the 11th century. His royal family started using the name after his death at the Battle of Clontarf in 1014, although it didn't come into general use until many years later. Brien is derived from the Irish *bran*, which means raven, although some sources believe it is more likely to have been derived from the word *brion*, meaning lofty or eminent.

The name has belonged to numerous illustrious people, many of whom had connections with counties Clare and Limerick, traditionally the O'Brien stronghold. O'Brien's Castle in Limerick city was probably the palace of the royal family of Thomond in the 13th century. In Co. Clare, Corcomroe Abbey, near Ballyvaughan, was founded by King Donal O'Brien in 1181. Today, Conor O'Brien, the 18th Baron Inchiquin, the O'Brien of Thomond and a direct descendant of Brian Boru, lives on the Dromoland estate near Newmarket-on-Fergus in Co. Clare.

O'Byrne

The O'Byrnes derive their ancestry from King Milesius, who came from Spain to Ireland in 558 B.C., and his son Heremon. The O'Byrne name itself is derived from *bran*, Irish for raven. It has long been a leading sept in east Leinster and is now one of the most numerous names in Ireland. Byrne is a derivative.

In Co. Wicklow, homeland of the O'Byrnes, the remains of Black Castle can be seen on the cliff edge at Wicklow town. This castle was a successor to that built in 1169 by Maurice Fitzgerald, an Anglo-Norman, to try and keep the O'Byrne chieftains at bay, because they were constantly raiding the town. One of the clan, Fiach MacHugh O'Byrne (1544–1597), then the clan chieftain, defeated an English army under Lord Gray at Glenmalure, near the great mountain of Lugnaquilla. The site of the battle can still be seen.

Two Byrnes are prominent in show business, Gay Byrne, the Irish broadcaster, and Gabriel Byrne, the Hollywood film actor, both of whom were born and brought up in Dublin.

O'Connell

O' Connell is one of the most famous names in Irish history. The O'Connells can trace their ancestry back to Eremonium Aengus Tuirneach, who was High King of Ireland in about 280 B.C. There were three distinct septs, in Co. Derry, in Co. Galway and, most importantly, in Co. Kerry, where it is one of the leading septs.

In Co. Kerry, the name is still prevalent. The Kerry O'Connells always had a broad European outlook, and this was evident in the most famous O'Connell, Daniel O'Connell, known as the Liberator, who was born near Cahirciveen in 1775 and died in Genoa in 1847. He conducted many crusades, most notably and successfully for Catholic Emancipation in Ireland in 1829.

The ruins of his birthplace can be seen just outside Cahirciveen, while his great house and estate at Caherdaniel in Co. Kerry are well preserved, with many mementoes in the house. The estate and house can be freely visited. The O'Connell Monument in O'Connell Street, Dublin, are both named in his honour.

O'Conor

The O'Conor clan is one of the most influential in Irish history. In Irish, the name is *Ó Conchobhair* or *O Conchúir*, from the personal name meaning champion. There are six distinct septs, with the Connacht and Kerry ones being the most important. The Connacht sept included High Kings of Ireland, the last of whom, Rory, was born in Castlerea, Co. Roscommon, in the 12th century. He died in 1198 and is buried at Clonmacnoise.

Clonalis House in Co. Roscommon is the ancestral seat of these O'Conors, whose ancestry included 11 High Kings of Ireland and 24 Kings of Connacht. The magnificent house contains many priceless treasures relating to the O'Conors and is open to the public.

Ballintober Castle, near Castlerea, was the stronghold of the O'Conors of Connacht from the early 14th to the 17th centuries. In Co. Kerry, Carrigafoyle Castle, built in 1490 by the chieftain Conor O'Connor, was the stronghold of the Kerry O'Connors. Denis O'Conor is the present O'Conor Don, the head of the family, who claims direct ancestry from the High Kings of Ireland.

O'Donnell

The name O'Donnell comes from *domnhaill*, which means world mighty; it was a popular Irish personal name.

The main sept of the O'Donnells is associated with Tirconnell in Co. Donegal, and the family also has links with counties Clare and Galway. Red Hugh O'Donnell, the most famous of the clan, lived from about 1571 to 1602. He was the Earl of Tyrconnell and was closely involved with the ill-fated struggle against the English at the end of the 16th century, which resulted in the exile of the Irish chiefs (known as the Wild Geese). In Donegal town, the castle, now largely restored, was the O'Donnell stronghold.

One of the descendants of the Wild Geese was Leopoldo O'Donnell (1809–1867), a prime minister of Spain, and the Spanish connection remains important. The sole surviving member of the O'Donnells of Tirconnel is Father Aedh O Donel, born in 1940, a Franciscan missionary in Zimbabwe. The head of the clan will pass from him to Spanish cousins, the Dukes of Tetuan.

O'Farrell

The O'Farrells are connected with Co. Longford. The name comes from the Irish *Ó Fearghaill*, which means a man of great courage. They were an important sept in territory known as Annaly in Co. Longford. Their seat was the site of present-day Longford town, which itself was known as Annaly until 1547. Longford owes its origins to an ancient castle of the Princes of Annaly, and the O'Farrells also founded a Dominican priory in the town in 1400. There is now no trace of either building.

When Richard O Ferrall married a Letitia More, they founded their own illustrious sept, the More O'Ferralls, who later became prominent in the world of television and advertising. George More O'Ferrall was an influential early TV and film producer in Britain; the More O'Ferralls also owned the More O'Ferrall outdoor advertising company, one of the largest of its kind in Britain and Ireland.

O'Ferrall is a variant of O'Farrell.

O'Kelly

The first bearer of the name O'Kelly was Ceallach, son of Finnachta, a chieftain of the people of Hy Many c. A.D. 874. *Ceallach* means war or contention. For centuries, they were one of the most powerful families in Connacht, mainly in counties Galway and Roscommon. Kilconnell Abbey, near Aughrim in Co. Galway, was founded by the O'Kellys in the early 15th century and its ruins are still extensive. There is also an ancient O'Kelly castle on the shores of Lough Conn in Co. Mayo.

Ned Kelly, the notorious Australian outlaw who died in 1880, had Irish connections: his father, Red Kelly, came from Tipperary town. Gene Kelly, born in 1912 in Philadelphia, was Irish on both sides of his family; he became renowned in Hollywood as a singer and dancer. Grace Kelly (1929–1982), also from Philadelphia, had outstanding success as a Hollywood film actress before marrying Prince Rainier of Monaco and becoming Princess Grace of Monaco. Her grandfather was an Irish immigrant; she traced her roots to near Newport, Co. Mayo.

O'Mahony

The O'Mahony name comes from Mathghamhan, son of Cian Mac Mael Muda, a 10th-century prince, and his wife Sadbh, daughter of the Irish High King Brian Boru. The O'Mahonys have always been particularly prominent in Munster, especially in Co. Cork, where their castles were strung out along the coastline as far west as Mizen Head. Many O'Mahonys still live there.

Among the prominent names in the clan was John O'Mahony (1816–1877), from Kilbeheny, near Mitchelstown in Co. Cork, who was cofounder of the Fenian movement. Also in the 19th century, the renowned Fr Francis O'Mahony, known as "Father Prout" was the author of such works as *The Bells of Shandon*. Eoin O'Mahony (1904–1970) was a barrister by profession, a great raconteur and broadcaster, who frequently discussed clan history on the radio; he was a familiar bearded figure travelling the roads of Ireland.

Today, the chief representative of the O'Mahony clan in Europe is Vicomte Yves O'Mahony of Orléans, France.

O'Neill

The O'Neills can trace their family history back to A.D. 360, a rare feat among the families of Europe. They are descended from the royal family of Tara, who were kings of Ulster and monarchs of all Ireland from the 5th to the early 17th centuries. The name comes from Nial Glún Dubh, or Niall of the Black Knee, who was a King of Ireland from 890 until he was killed in 919. His grandson Domhnall adopted the surname Neill, which means champion. In addition to the O'Neills of Ulster, where the family is most numerous, there are septs in Thomond (counties Clare and Limerick), Decies (Co. Waterford), and Co. Carlow.

The name is distinguished both within and beyond Ireland. Hugh O'Neill (1550–1616), the Second Earl of Tyrone, was defeated by the English at the battle of Kinsale in 1601. He was the last great leader of Gaelic Ireland. But in 1646, Owen Roe O'Neill defeated an English and Scottish army at Benburb, Co. Tyrone. Much material on the O'Neills can be found in the O'Neill historical centre there.

O'Reilly

The name O'Reilly comes from the Irish chieftain Ragheallach, who lived at the time of Brian Boru and, like him, was killed at the Battle of Clontarf in 1014. He was a great-grandson of Maomordha, a descendant of the O'Conors, kings of Connacht. Today, it is one of the most numerous names in Ireland.

Co. Cavan is a particular stronghold of the name. Myles "The Slasher" O'Reilly was the heroic defender of the bridge at Finea in Co. Cavan in 1646 where he and a force of one hundred held out against a 1,000-strong Cromwellian army. O'Reilly is commemorated by a cross in the main street of Finea, a pretty village on the banks of the River Inny.

The most famous holder of the name today is Dr. A. J. F. O'Reilly, the wealthiest man in Ireland. He is the head of the Heinz Corporation and Independent Newspapers, Dublin, and used to play rugby for Ireland.

O'Sullivan

This name is from the Irish *Suilleabhain*, which means one-eyed or hawk-eyed, and is particularly widespread in counties Cork and Kerry.

Dunboy Castle at Castletownbere, on the Beara peninsula in Co. Cork, was the home of the O'Sullivan Beare, the chief of the O'Sullivans. Under Donall O'Sullivan Beare, it was the last stronghold in Munster to hold out for Philip of Spain against the English forces after the defeat of the Irish and the Spanish at the Battle of Kinsale in 1601. Dunboy Castle was finally destroyed in 1602; the garrison refused to surrender until the walls were shattered. The annual O'Sullivan clan gathering is held in Castletownbere every June.

In the 18th century Owen Roe O'Neill, whose work as a teacher was constantly interrupted by his womanising, was a great lyric poet. Maureen O'Sullivan, born in Boyle, Co. Roscommon, had a distinguished Hollywood acting career. She is probably best known for her role as Jane, playing opposite Johnny Weismuller in the *Tarzan* films of the 1930s and 1940s.

Power

The name Power is originally Norman. It may have come from the old French word *poore*, meaning poor, or from *Pohier*, meaning a native of the town of Pois, in Picardy, France. The Powers came to Ireland in the 12th century with the Anglo-Norman invasion, and the clan became among the most Hibernicised of all the Anglo-Norman families. Today, it is principally found in and around Co. Waterford.

Among the places associated with the name is Curraghmore House, near Kilmacthomas in west Waterford. In the 18th century, James Power, Earl of Tyrone, rebuilt the house and laid out gardens on a scale to match Versailles. The 8th Marquis of Waterford still lives in Curraghmore House, a treasure trove of Power family history.

The estate at Powerscourt, near Enniskerry in Co. Wicklow, was originally granted to a Norman knight, Eustace le Poer, after the Anglo-Norman invasion. A castle was built there by William Power, probably in the 15th century, which was demolished to make way for Powerscourt House in the 18th century.

Roche

The Roches originally came from Flanders, then emigrated to Pembrokeshire in Wales, before three of the family—David, Adam and Henry de la Roch—joined Strongbow in the Anglo-Norman invasion of Ireland in the 12th century. At Glanworth, near Fermoy in Co. Cork, can be seen the ruins of a Roche castle destroyed by Cromwellian forces in the 17th century. West of Glanworth is the attractive village of Castletownroche, which derives its name from another Roche settlement. A more complete Roche castle can be seen in Co. Wexford—the Norman castle at Ferrycarrig, now the location of the Irish National Heritage Park. In all there are sixteen Rochestowns in Ireland and innumerable Roche castles.

Some of the best-known names of the present day have sporting connections, notably Stephen Roche, born in Dublin in 1959. A champion cyclist, he won the Tour de France and the world championship in 1987.

A Roche clan rally is held every year in June.

Ryan

The Ryans are descended from a 2nd century King of Leinster, Cathaoir Mór. The meaning of the name remains uncertain, but it may mean illustrious. The Irish version of the name, *Ó Maoilriain*, from the main Ryan sept, is now usually abbreviated to *Ó Riain*, the name of the small Leinster sept of the Ryans. Other anglicised versions of the name include Mulryan in Co. Tipperary and O'Ryan in Co. Carlow.

Among the holders of the name were Cornelius Ryan (1920–1974), born in Synge Street, Dublin, who became a war correspondent during the World War II and subsequently wrote *The Longest Day*, about the D-Day landings in 1944. In sports, Ken Ryan has been secretary-general of the Olympic Council of Ireland since 1976, while Paddy Ryan (born in Pallasgreen, Co. Limerick in 1883), emigrated to the United States where he became an Olympic hammer thrower for his adopted country.

Sheridan

S heridans are descendants of *O Sioradáin*, but no records exist of who this was. Little more is known about the Sheridans than that their roots are in Co. Cavan. Literature has been the abiding talent of the Sheridans. Richard Brinsley Sheridan (1751–1816), the dramatist, was born in Dublin but fashioned his theatrical career in London. In the 19th century, Joseph Sheridan Le Fanu (1814–1873) wrote novels based on the supernatural that inspired Bram Stroker to create *Dracula*. Margaret Burke Sheridan, born in Castlebar, Co. Mayo, became Ireland's first prima donna. In the great Italian opera houses, her singing was considered totally Italian in style, but she died in relative obscurity in 1958.

Of the all the Sheridans, the one who contributed most to humanity's enjoyment of life was a Dublin chef called Joe Sheridan. During World War II he was working at the Foynes seaplane base on the Shannon estuary. One day in 1943, to warm up some passengers who had been delayed, he invented Irish Coffee, ·a mixture of coffee, Irish whiskey, and cream.

Smith

Comparatively little is known about the history of this family name in Ireland, which is as commonplace in England as Murphy is in Ireland. Its Irish equivalent is MacGouran, which means son of the smith. It came to Ireland with the English and Scottish planters who settled in Ulster and also with the Cromwellian soldiers who came to Ireland in the mid-17th century. The name is particularly numerous in Co. Cavan.

There are few prominent locations associated with this name. Smith Hill, in Co. Roscommon, is one mile north-west of Elphin and may have been the birthplace of Oliver Goldsmith, the 18th-century dramatist. His grandfather, who had his house here, was the local curate. In the previous century Erasmus Smith (1611–1691) was a wealthy man who founded the Erasmus Smith grammar schools in Ireland, the first endowed schools of their kind.

Walsh

W alsh is the fourth most popular family name in Ireland, but the Walshs do not have a common ancestor. The name derives from the Welshmen who came to Ireland in the 12th century with the Anglo-Norman invasion. It is common all over the country, but especially in the south-east, in Waterford city and county. There, it is often pronounced "Welsh," true to its origins.

Among the famous Walshs was Maurice Walsh, the former customs officer, who wrote *The Quiet Man*, an Oscar-winning film whose cast included Maureen O'Hara and John Wayne. Other and earlier Walshs included Thomas FitzAnthony Walsh, who was the Governor of Leinster in the 13th century. He built the fortifications at Thomastown, Co. Kilkenny, fragments of which can still be seen today, together with the nearby Grenan Castle, now in ruins. Father Michael Walsh (1828–1866) was the parish priest of Sneem, Co. Kerry, and the "Father O'Flynn" of the famous song.

The Walshs have no clan head and, although the name is so widespread, there is no clan seat.

Index of Names